The Lady Who Loved Chimpanzees

The Jane Goodall Story

Biography 4th Grade
Children's Women Biographies

BABY PROFESSOR

EDUCATION KIDS

Speedy Publishing LLC
40 E. Main St. #1156
Newark, DE 19711
www.speedypublishing.com

In this book, we're going to cover the fascinating life of animal rights activist and ethologist Jane Goodall. So, let's get right to it!

WHO IS JANE GOODALL?

Jane Goodall is an animal rights activist and an ethologist. Animal rights activists hold the view that animals should be protected and not harmed or killed in ways that cause the animals extreme pain. Ethologists study animal behavior. Jane has spent her life studying the behavior of chimpanzees in the wild.

Dr. Jane Goodall with FiFi,
Gombe National Park, Tanzania

Since chimpanzees are primates and humans are also primates, studying their behavior also impacts anthropology, the study of human behavior. There is only a 1.2% genetic difference between modern humans and chimpanzees. Jane's studies of chimpanzees have uncovered a great deal of scientific discoveries and, as a result, she's well known and highly respected worldwide.

EARLY LIFE

Born in 1934 in London, England, Jane was destined to have an adventurous life. Her father, Mortimer Herbert Goodall, was a businessman with a love for racing cars. Her mother, Margaret Myfanwe Joseph, was an author and wrote novels under the pen name Vanne Morris Goodall.

STORY by Emma Wildsmith

primal
instincts

now in her seventies, renowned primatologist Jane
Goodall is fighting harder than ever for a better future

Jane and her sister Judy spent their early years in London as well as Bournemouth. Very early on, she became fascinated with animals and their behavior. Her father gave her a chimpanzee toy, which he named "Jubilee." It sparked her interest in animals.

As she wandered the seaside resort town of Bournemouth, she observed the native animals and made detailed notes and sketches. She was an avid reader and soaked up everything she could get on zoology as well as ethology. She started to dream about going to Africa where she could see fascinating animals in their natural environments.

EARLY INTEREST IN PRIMATE BEHAVIOR

Jane was a student at the Uplands private school. In 1950, she received her certificate and received a second certificate two years later. She was only 18 years old when she left school and got a job at the prestigious Oxford University.

She was saving to make a trip to Africa and to make more money she was working additional hours at a film company that was making documentary films. Then she got her first big break on her way to working full-time in Africa.

A friend from her childhood invited her to visit Kenya. From there, through some other friends, she met the world-famous anthropologist Louis Leakey. At that time, he was the curator of the Coryndon Museum, located in Nairobi.

Seeing her enthusiasm for ethology, Leakey hired her to be a secretary so she could participate in the work he was doing. He also invited her to come to an exciting archaeological dig. This dig was at Olduvai Gorge, which was filled with prehistoric fossil remains of early humans.

Jane was so excited by the work that was being done at Olduvai. She also went to Africa's largest freshwater lake to study the vervet monkeys that were living on an island there.

WHY LEAKEY SELECTED GOODALL

It was Leakey's belief that studies of the higher primates and their behavior would lead to important information that could be used to understand how humans evolved. He was very interested in chimpanzees since they were thought to be the second most intelligent, nonhuman primates.

However, at that time there had been almost no successful studies of chimpanzees. Observers didn't have what it took to stay out in the field with the chimps long enough to accurately document their behavior. Sometimes the size of the group on safari scared the chimps into unnatural behaviors.

Leakey had faith in Goodall. He thought she had the persistence to endure isolation in the wild with the chimps for a long enough time to observe their real behaviors. Many people didn't agree with his choice of Goodall, since she didn't have a college degree or any formal training in science.

GOODALL'S OBSERVATIONS OF CHIMPS IN AFRICA

Leakey set to work to get the needed funds for the Gombe Reserve project he wanted for Jane to take on. In the meantime, Jane went back to England to work on a documentary about animals.

In 1960, at the age of 26 in the company of her mother and a cook from Africa, she set up camp at the shore of Lake Tanganyika located at the Gombe Stream Reserve. At the beginning, she couldn't get within 500 yards of the families of chimps, but Jane was patient and soon thought of a plan.

She started to appear every day at the same time and location and soon the chimps got used to her being there. Within a year, she was able to observe them from only 30 feet away. Within two years, they would come to her to get bananas!

GOODALL'S AMAZING DISCOVERIES

Jane called her daily feeding of the chimps the "banana club." As she gained their trust, she became very familiar with the over 100 chimps that lived on the reserve. She blended in by imitating their behaviors and spending time in trees. She even ate some of the same foods to fit in with their societies. Because she observed the chimps so closely for such a long period of time she made many new discoveries.

Some of the discoveries Jane made were:

* Chimps have a complicated social system.
* They have a primitive sound language made up of 20 different sounds.
* They use hugs to comfort one another and have long-term bonds within their families.
* The dominant males are the most powerful in the group. Other less dominant males and females try to "play nice" with these males so they will not be harmed by them. The male chimps don't actively participate in the "family life" types of behaviors.
* They're not vegetarians as was widely thought. They eat large insects as well as birds. On occasion they would hunt small baboons and antelope to eat.
* In some circumstances, chimps have been known to eat other chimps, which is called cannibalism.

E GOODALL

MISS GOODALL AND THE WILD CHIMPANZEES

Jane loved her life with the chimps but it was isolated out there in the wild.

In 1962, the National Geographic Society sent a wildlife photographer and filmmaker to do a documentary of Jane at work. His name was Baron Hugo van Lawick. While he was there, the two fell in love and they married in March of 1964. It was one of the few rare times when Jane was away from her chimps.

She also made trips to Cambridge University so that she could receive her doctorate in ethology in 1965. Even though she didn't have a bachelor's degree, she was still able to pursue her Ph.D.

She was only the eighth person in Cambridge's history to accomplish this. She wrote her thesis about the behavior of the wild chimpanzees. In 1965, her work became known worldwide when her husband's film, Miss Goodall and the Wild Chimpanzees, was shown on American TV.

chka
GLS Bank
das macht Sinn
BAUM
GLS
uture Co
Hausch

The couple and their young son, Hugo Jr., who was born in 1967, soon were well known in both the US and Britain. Jane challenged scientists everywhere to rethink their ideas about what humans and other primates had in common.

IN THE SHADOW OF MAN

Throughout her life, Jane has continued to publish articles and books that described her discoveries. In 1971, she published In the Shadow of Man. This text not only offered her scientific notes but also entertained readers with its descriptions of the human-like events in chimp families.

Chimpanzee

In 1973, she began a position at University of Dar es Salaam located in Tanzania as a visiting Zoology professor. Her first marriage ended in divorce and she married Derek Bryceson in 1975. Bryceson was the director of the Tanzania national parks.

After attending a conference in Chicago in 1986 centering on the need for chimps to be treated ethically, Jane turned her attention to exposing the inhuman treatment of chimps for research as well as the dangers chimpanzees face in a shrinking habitat.

my way PREISTRÄGER
Prof. Dr. Christiaan Bernard
Herzspender
2000
2001
2002
Präsident Lech Wałęsa
2003
Erwin Kräutler
Bischof und Missionar
2012
2005
2015
my way

In 1989, she published a book for children called The Chimpanzee Family Book. The book received an award from UNESCO for children's book of the year. With the prize money she received, she had the book translated into Swahili. She had copies distributed around areas where chimps live to raise awareness of the need for conserving chimp habitats.

ACCOMPLISHMENTS

Now in her eighties, Jane continues to work to encourage scientists to find other ways to research without inflicting pain on animals. She doesn't believe in destructive demonstrations, but instead believes that militant animal activists defeat their cause with violence. Throughout her lifetime, she's received many awards and continues to write about and champion humane treatment for primates and other animals.

Now you know more about Jane Goodall's life, her interesting work with chimpanzees, and her stand on the rights of animals. You can find more Biographies about Famous Women from Baby Professor by searching the website of your favorite book retailer.

Visit
BABY PROFESSOR
EDUCATION KIDS
www.BabyProfessorBooks.com
to download Free Baby Professor eBooks
and view our catalog of new and exciting
Children's Books